escape artist

contents

escape artist

Kate Hammerich

ISBN 978-1-4303-1297-0

For my mom

Thank you to everyone who held out a hand.

escape artist

she climbed the stairs

the stars break the dark
as if words have not yet been invented

if only i could catch my breath

the steps are cold under my bare feet
my bones are melting into my skin

i have folded myself

    into the backseat
dreaming

our revolution rises
from under the covers

speaking a language we have forgotten
speaking in your voice

we sign a temporary cease fire at
4am
    and roll from the warmth
to start the day

i am a man of parts
i am a woman of words

leaving notes on the dark breakfast table
dirty dishes filling the sink

outside
the dew lifts
    fog breaking
with impossible speed

if i do not write i will die

you disappear into the morning sun
    blinding

i no longer know your name
or face

where will i sleep when you are gone?

balcony

from the start
i have known you
              and so i can't forgive you
anything

it is what it is
what shapes us

you were here when i woke up
           and i imagine you not leaving until tomorrow

i imagine you not leaving

soothed by the pressure of my forehead on your freckled
shoulder
the shifting of muscle and bone

because you breathe, you are beautiful

i have thought of your face
the sincere tilt of nose and impossible promises to
   become a more accurate version of self

in-between times
we build homes with laughter
places to return to

the moonlight creeps up the wall
             spilling over the sill
burning the white walls
with a reflection of a reflection of the day

the birds in the median stretch restless wings
and murmur to each other

but because the wind has not deserted us
the maple trees flash the silver underside of their leaves
calling the rain

i give you back your days of air conditioned silence
your literature, your clean dishes

your skylight

i have known you
              and so i can for you give
anything

god is in the rain

we are planning our failures
and

like water

you spill
freely

from my heart

you rose like bread in the morning
warm-scented and earthy

and for a moment i had you
in a quiet kitchen
flooded with light

before trembling like a kite-string
        climbing into restricted
                        air-space
you form a brief sentence in which you use both
fate
      and farewell

impossible

still
that breath is in my mouth

extending

brilliant and unsure
as our finger's touch

but
when i said forever
unfortunately
      i meant it

and we
stray

silence

in your cadence
i cannot grow

this conversation we never had
hanging accusingly
in the air waves

rain caressing the windows

between here and there
lightning-struck

i am
falling forward

alone

a cage left open

the only answer in the world

the only answer in the world

is: momentum

will i ever know the whole truth

  my hands grow to match my mother's
my wrists age

crumbling in the darkness
at your irreparable touch

a sharp breeze
      like cool fingers
  sliding easy
under
my sweater

the things i cannot deny

  does he change you
in the obscurity of
morning

are your words echoed back
  over
and over

this unspoken
audience
of need

this overwhelming
death
that will not be
satisfied

once again i fail to see the connection

your hands go through me as i'm trying to think back on a better
time

pointing out the things that i won't resist
we were lost and stuck together

voices
scattering
away

            and

i’m not going to forget

it is difficult to rise each morning with a kind heart
but everything has to start somewhere

the ground is spongy and welcomes our feet
and this is still a private war

we peel the tangerines from opposite sides of the table
bright orange petals under strong unwatched hands
guarded and guarding
                                        vigilant for the answer when it comes

how we learn to bear our selves
excuse our happiness
our thriving
                      our desire

i reach out and praise you with my hands
with my ears
                         tuned
for the danger hurling past
  just
                       out of reach

(high) speed

folded tightly into
appropriate responses

we are surrounded by silence

and   we have made a religion
out of waiting

while i
(always the sacrifice)

find you here
in the plastic taste of cherry chapstick

unhealing
self-interest

our creator hides under a Stetson
delighting
in the round slow sounds of speech

divination
                    lost

to the sunlight

withdrawal

when the war comes how will we prepare

you told me what love was and
i believed you

pencils lining
the drawers of words and charcoal sketches
without perspective

take the night off and let's drive
past weekend traffic

through sand and water dreams
i've become a ghost before my eyes

or how

i wish i hated it here so i could leave
i wish the sun would reach past the barrier of skin
and light my insides

the hand of the wind guiding me

sometimes the door opens
and people just walk in

the steps are simple

the way your hand felt when we were sober
as if i hadn't been touched for
years

as if it were only
yesterday
you followed desire into the backseat

we are willing to die
for the good times

for the trees projecting shadows on a face
green
          into light

when the walls are too thin to keep your voice out
and you remember you don't care

until tomorrow

iconography

how can we live every day in fear
we may be some sort of crazy

to be swallowed in the numbness of

the shadow of my shadow

cutting hair and fingers
twisted together

counting, counting

we are saved by
the symmetry of days

        and memory loss

sleepless
in windswept dark

moonlight steals my house
and gives me holes in return

illuminates the gaps in our honesty
the escape plan

a white hand on a white wall
love of me with your bones and skin

i am a night gardener
cultivating the fragile
            insurmountable
petals of your heart

for all the rules i learned to accept
i will not forgive myself

under your psalms i am sinning

fleetingly

i fling myself into the void

(in your silence
always

i remember)

down the sullen street
the candy glow

the push
of pragmatic shoppers
how i search for you

in the empty sea

the fog moves on your
breath

less
my pride
my unquenchable rage

exploding like a bombshell
(the one we promised to hold on to
forever)

she listened by my side
without knowing the truth
(without knowing you)

time swelled
so unexpectedly
we have been free

and we are too curious
        to know eternal glory

but
yesterday
        i saw a unicorn
 in the neighbour's field
                waiting

becoming

my mother is bright

in dark

addictive glow
 rising

i see her face in my mirror
unspeakable y
beautiful

and wordless
  we speak in
tongues

about how
in dreams i gather her
 into
myself

as if we had always been returning
home

promise

the soap glistens on your skin

black and white
gravure

a pictured pose
of the girl you intended to be

dreaming.
they've all been forgetting and
                                        i have
not

yesterday, today
some other early morning

you pass through me
and enter my dreams

unravel your past
like silk-spun fairy tales

tomorrow rippling uncertain
   (just out of reach)

and someday we will be alone

confess your sins

confess

in
speaking words

dull bound books
stacked
mysterious

as morning rose high
against the crumbling walls

your

silences strewn
between
two kite strings
taut
and torn

breath
less

sins
of the flesh

tremble on the cusp
between clinical and

exquisite
temptations

your hands lay over mine

compulsion

my name is not safe anymore
but a sound that causes my selves
to
                        panic

we open
and unopen
the door

the lock is slick under my fingers

the shutter
                     stop

   counting violet breaths

under my breath

they change to grey and gold
          and enter the sunlight easily

which answers the question of tomorrow

rites of passage
my words placed carefully on a page

i lie with my hair in my hand on Tuesdays
         and under a pillow on Friday

my freckles are wrinkled
i hear your feet inside the wall
the refrigerator turns on and sleep comes for me

rituals of safety
carefully disorganized
for the casual eye

the hunger passing sense
becoming lightness
                      a permission to cut dinner in one hundred pieces
the last bite with closed eyes

the headache throbs
waiting
          traveling around my skull

waiting

for me to put down the pencil
and let him in

there is a poem in every third breath
a sonnet, a song

but i cannot hear them past the white light

my brain is devouring itself
in one hundred pieces

                    i dare not close my eyes

waves crash on the shore and we play
who can reach farther into
the unknown depths

i imagine worlds i have never seen
i see you at the place where i lost myself

it's a long story
she says
so i'll just tell you the end

out the door
and in the backyard
you were waiting
waiting

inevitable

crawling up from places
unseen

spinning out of reach

and it is so easy to forget who it is
in the dark of the night

embark

your back curves away from me
smooth and
            shaded with warmth

uncharted waters
and your sleeping breaths

you have amended these things
these broken wings

          flightless dreams

meaning
              creeps
in
unnoticed

incontrovertibly
lovely

your fingers speak
        in foreign tongues

only the angle of my bones
        and contours of unlit skin
comprehend

(remember i won't be able to forgive you for everything)

you turn a blind eye
          to our possibilities

like the li[f]eli[n]es of your palm
that i know so well

we circle

looking for weaknesses

the tiniest movement
(and i hand you my heart)

my joy and grief

the light imprisons me
bars of gold

i am blended in colours
hiding in the tall grass
self-righteous blades

you are not my enemy
but you wear his face

lightly masking
your intent

i bow to you my father
the Sun
all of our ghosts

you pacifists
polishing your electric chairs

past 7th Avenue
stretching memories over my fragile body

Orion on a clear night
the murmuring frogs

i will keep going until i run out of places to go

as if this was all i ever wanted
as if the world were waiting to let us down

we make love on a sunny afternoon
War & Peace
with its broken spine
under the swing

you do not look me in the eye
because our secrets are contagious

and some days
i do not want to fly
or dream of better things

i only want to take your hand
and remember the mornings

that stretched into the horizon
endlessly

petals

loam
being the softest
of words

tentatively
               rolling
in the back of your throat

deep dusky
recesses

under pink tipped trees

muted and
waking from a dream

of you
pink tipped

and smiling
   only for me

the daffodil version of we
i sometimes remember
to forget

earth-turned
barefoot

soft and unspoken
you lie between us

dawn
       rising
               clear

as sunshine
        that asks nothing

and means nothing
   (but the slow turning

of the world)

and everything

i know what i want

for Jettison

if we aren't more specific
how am i ever going to know what to say

  how am i going to learn how to be
alone

though,
      (you'll never leave me)

    and even if i use the wrong words
it still means the same thing

like new flowers in the garden
we are blossoming
                    -    blossoming

under the rainbow spray
         spilling out of your mouth like songs

riding the wind

unspoken

joy!
joy!

pine scented fury
rushes in sparks

flaring towards the sky

(convince me)

in changes you hide
unmistakable

irreverent—

tired, tired

in need of so many thorns

who do we ask for forgiveness?

torn

... still

the floor
the floor

rises up to greet me

like dropping
into
sleep

while the road curves
darkly

in front

i watch you fall

awake

escape artist

their headlights caress the wet pavement -
you speak to me in jakob dylan's voice

disassembled and alive

the vibrant sulfur of ginkgo clinging to the bricks

and
our telescopes reveal questions

remembering a summer evening that trembled
faintly hummed

insatiable

with the escalating urgency of
tomorrow

though
the pictures were dark

you claimed beauty with unexpected clairvoyance

in the muted sunlight of autumn's conclusions
we hug awkwardly

and for the first time
you realize i might not make it

sorting through the subtle phrases to find the key
you hide answers in my most neglected places

liars

as if you have all the time in the world
you just lie with me
        and we forget the war

and the clouds climb the stairs
like mannequins

they climb the mountains by
tree-tip

spiderwebs of rain
opening

your arms

when you swallowed the sky
you invented an alternate future for me

        (i keep it in my bottom drawer)

witch hunter

i have already forgotten your hands
but not your voice
      never
                        never

echoing back at me
like a plague

i clean again, and wait

narcissus trembling, silent and watchful in the still pond
the clouds unfurling across the sky

you are growing inside of me
like a thought

your dim whispering
slender and
         controversial

weighting the palm of my hand
       the rock proving that you don't float and maybe

just maybe

you were innocent after all

star

my crazy thoughts
    a summer day

sun

high and
        hazed

bleached

the way the water is the same white as the sky
as you dip your toes into imaginary clouds

knowing
a monster is curled
beneath the drug sculpture

in the peopled cities   you look away
unnoticeably

your laughter
a five-pointed star
bouncing back to its
own
center

you always used cloth bandages
so you could iron them slow
humming to your headphones
as you pressed them slowly into perfection

we are the same colour blue, carefully folding
desires

the private lie

and even though we promised to be through
she can't let go of you

cabbage moths

she says
   anything
 is
                 possible

no.

anything is possible
        (anywhere but here will do)

but

to believe
in you
is a task

not for the faint of heart
or breath

you fall
       under

pressure

mind's
dark demands

                  - a moment of doubt

coming through a door
          left open

i dream in colours
        i colour in dreams
that you give me

black and white lines
naming your demands

one airplane
    a few million

miles of
sky

they are
white like moons
in the stillness of
        afternoon
carelessly dropping
fairydust
on trembling petals

flutter
            flutter

rest

wait ...

                    liftoff!

Miss America

crawling like ants
over the dark roll of highway

i remember how small this country really is
North Carolina
   to California
spilling under me

breathless and blue
the honest mountains stand

and
you are still
     the most beautiful thing
          I have ever seen

not because of the slope or
proportionality of your perfect limbs

the ocean shades your eyes

i hear the rise and
fall
of your laugh

       breeching a freckle spattered nose
                                   tumbling

into the silences

only the good die young

the problem with escaping
is that you might end up someplace worse

after all this life is a complete mess

remember the way she looked at you
when she knew -

and your thoughts covered your face

(my thoughts, of course, were never on my face,
but they often came out my mouth)

so you

borrow a slow moving conversation
carry it into another room

where the sun shines on linoleum
and there are snippets of Hemmingway in the air

you remember Cezanne, hungry and brilliant

the accumulation of intellect covering the anger
you worked so hard to destroy

but you knew

this world was always better for writing
than living

lacking answers

we're all here waiting for a future
that got lost along the way

where life begins

we
 siesta

in sweltering noon

honey
      drops

tension

fascination
evaluating every step

        (you wait here)

when you are broken
you become stronger

healing like a bone
splintered and splinted

your two-dimensional
smile

unhinging

            my knees

faceted
around your waist

swinging on

how
this music tells me
nothing

but the mistakes
i've made

today

conversations
rolling

down

while
you scream,
believing you are someone
else

the air trembles
anticipation

your green eyes
blue skies

dreams of better times

(you know im lying
half the time)

i don't kiss you on the street to be political
    or to make a statement

i don't hold your hand for shock value

i kiss you, quietly, in front of the subway
because you are going away
    to somewhere i will not be able to reach

and my fingertips already ache
    with this separation

the taste of you dissolving swiftly from my lips

the crowds shifting and whispering around us
as if all of Chicago
    knows

your gold skin shivers under fluorescent lighting -
under the weight of your cruelty

    we have to say goodbye here

you say,
because you are meeting them
tonight
    because they don't even know my name

and your eyes can't keep secrets

dissonance

i yearn towards and
hate
                you

disconcerting
        contradictions

the gaps between
 thought
              and speech

your implications
     my imperfections

we dig in
         out of curiosity

in the air is always
your tension
misapprehension

the keys fall from
the door

a cold hand on your shoulder
and the world
knows

we wander away
with the trees underfoot

trusting
fire
            flies

hovering
           in
the semi-dark

exhausted

by the sun

lounging over everything

the sudden roll of
heat
lightning

(and i never knew my hips could move like that)
breathless

her fantasy
involved a waterfall of tequila

and all eyes were on me
but all i could think of was you

and how you
don't let me

down

dragging me
through
the days

suffocating under all this
freedom

turning
me

inside
out

wind in the willows

we wait, trembling
in a place we never belonged

(you have no business here)

joking about ourselves
        and the way we are

dancing
    like rain

torrents
pouring out
        the language of thoughts
rhythmic as
question and answer

we speak in silences

and
i am a stranger in a strange land
comforted
by your obscurity

liquid tension
    curved in your hand
palm on palm

and the willow knows all your secrets
but tells me nothing
            loyalty and love

the wind has mine
          she flings them everywhere
                      laughing

but yesterday she caressed the long limbs
of your tree

and we were still

brief

you
      or someone
uncertainly
like you

invading

                      my dreams

fragmented

and the wind
           with summer chill

suddenly

fingering the
base
of
my
spine

                          the resident owl hoots
low
             disconcertingly
demanding
in the pre-dusk light

and the cicadas respond with silence

momentarily

you look up and meet my eye

perhaps
remembering how
you tugged our clothes from the dryer
     a spill of red sweater

my yellow fuzzy socks

covered with
flakes of a Kleenex from
sadder times

(listen to me,
    i warned you)

while
you dance in soft rain showers
in coral petals
    powder-soft on lips

parted

and i wrote you a letter
that you never read

the guilt of bad intentions

closing your eyes as the light began to pour from my openings
unashamed

we set sail

between the lines

he sees through me
    sharply unapologetic

as i withdraw from the field
and pretend he does
                not hear

                the bottle opening silently
under the table

chained
to the wall

        hypnotized

laden
engaged
changed

like lithium she breathes deep from the
empty
        cans

delirious
    and pale

the moon pools into our hands

we are invaded
    brilliant and

the language tumbled from your
smiling mouth

when
she kissed me like a secret
    like time was not passing

and the miles had never fallen between us

sinister

her olive limbs stretch upwards
        pinpointing the break between
earth and sky

swirling her vacant leaves

red on dark

the night flaring up
into our hands

i am in love with a man who is afraid of me
   drifting
            aimless

(you went so pale, he said)

in your arms i am a dark fire
a broken limb

          grass swaying in the cloudy wind

i want to examine the inches of your skin

planes feathering into hollows
heated dark

                  forgotten

we avoid the gaps
          between then and now

you left me humming to myself
    tuneless

ruins

you pick the knots of my stitches
one by one

                    free

flames rise
and break the dark
to pieces

sparks

on days it rains
my voice
instinctively
speaks for you

stanzas
sharp
against the flat
of my tongue

the train splits the night
an invading cry

if i would have known then

i would have left
my fingers there

in your hair

tracing the fierce arches
of your spine

and blinded my eyes
against
the dark

between us

the shirt wraps my waist
tight, intense
as if it could hold my failing pieces
together

when morning
forgets
to arrive

coming silent

you turn your face towards the pale sky
rising

Stiles

for Tavis

in a different world
        i know your voice
instead of only the still-frame of your face
smiling out of a million pixels of colour

and i do not constantly imagine
how it was they found you

shredded into
strangers' hands

but here
cruelty
      shines like a flashlight
on a dark night

and we cling to thin wires
of love

tornadoes

if i danced
blindly
in the sun

would this all make sense
would i know what to do
suddenly

my pen
        is
        dangerous

as words

you apologize with a mouth
that has no sound

just a shape that keeps
changing

only
in your silence
am i forgiven

this is our war
fought on the sidelines

without propaganda
or posters

just our silences

batted back
and
forth

with unerring precision

purposeless

your spirit enters my house
like the ghost of the dead

and i wonder where you are

your heels click
immaculately
through the dust of a kitchen warmed by sunlight

openings of conversation

i dreamed of tornadoes
and the light behind

when will it be our time?

these 4 years

airplanes like
shooting
stars
through the violet dusk
of hand-holding and white t-shirts

the grass green-scented
waving

eyes closed

she is wearing half my headphones
a love-promise
of Tori Amos

singing

just another Dead Fag to you
just another Light missing

and we're
another four years closer to the[ir] answer

while
the virgin mary's on your porch

chipped blue plastic
fighting empty beercans

as you lie in your hammock
another naked girl
rising, nameless

another wasted year

your scent remembered
accidentally
on my skin
and im sorry for not loving you more
heterosexually

but you never made me
want
to

Oh -

apologize
        for missing our wedding

graduating to

swinging in my hammock
                        with another brown-eyed girl

finding my own answers

behind the prison tower

we are on a mission
from your god

you tremble under me
like a blank spot
an almost-remembered life

reincarnated

lost on a time line
between here and there

you are a shadow
in a broken dream

and im tired of your nightmares

night despairs
(you're night time)
      let the sun rise

you have been hiding around the corners
of my mind

and you won't be swayed by my words

                              but they are all i have

my handwriting falters
observing the world through (stained)glass
of your choosing

i am careful with you

my poet
my reader

you are
doubting that i will fight you
    but my nails are already chipped

and i have nothing left to lose

undoing

i shy away from the thought
that approached
like a clumsy ghost
on a quiet night

impossible to ignore

and as the hawk tumbled
to the ground
robin redbreast
trembling in his
dark grasp

i remembered how things really were
unsure

as if in a dream i
continue

and it is almost impossible to tell at this point, but we had all the time in the world

you were listening, then
unaware, uncertain, but wholly committed

what is it i am looking for in your pages?

you [refuse]
an answer
myself

every time i close my eyes
something changes

and maybe it's a lie
the way you turn
to me

carnival prizes
vices
        and your good intentions

until even i
believe
                                        something
is better than nothing

as if it mattered

for this the world
will not stop
turning

though her orbit may
readjust
to fit

our blank
        [spot]

the night
lacks oxygen

but
i am still here
    breathing

as the crow flies

the star of Bethlehem
        dips past Orion
hovering on the edge of the horizon
                        in   frigid detachment

unbalanced

your toes grip concrete
                        fiercely
the soft sweet arch of your skin on my skin
breathing harsh

caught desperate
insecure

the way your fingers find mine again and again
      surprising you

and if i say i can’t hear you i lied

(mmhmm, dear
            that’s nice)

allowing compliments
        to override honesty

we worship the vampire of dreams
            suck suck sucking
us dry
      nightly

(and call it love)

the groundspeed of joy

what kind of scale compares the weight of two beauties
the gravity of duties or the groundspeed of joy
- Ani Difranco

you would think i was making poetry

with the sun and the stars
the trees swaying under the painful blue

(i know she still turns and smiles at you)

holes
        in my memory

hesitations

rolling yourself
  downhill

snowballing

soft powder and the unexpected glint
of ice

hard things

picking up speed
her red lights glare at me as she rounds the corner

reflections of planes
            throwing themselves at the sky

roaring

i record over last month's tape
old words dissolving under my confident mouth

at a slow party
you whisper in my ear

a crack in the wall   the backdoor

while the tangy scent of the iron staircase
stains my palms

watching the pale sky
    blue with city living
even as yesterday falls into
                        today

i kissed you
     under Van Gogh
 under the impression
we meant something

more than this

vertigo

you dream
twitching

a long
pause between
breath
and life

long-fingered

grasping for something past me
out of reach

anatomy breaks us into pieces
precisely labeled digits
who would not recognize themselves

in the hollows of your heart
the echoes vibrate
uninterrupted

in the dark
i have lost my direction
slipping a foot forward
tentative

holding breath
plunging over
the unexpected

the last step

of stomach dropping

awakening

eulogy

for dani

rising,
   into my arms
like a wave

eager
   evaporating

            breathless

the door bell rings

disturbing the
         pieces

(there was no one at the door besides, perhaps, a better decision
that will leave me just as lonely as you)

and turning back
you have been
misplaced

it is not fear
that makes me need more
or less
than your perfection

but everything,
     it seems,
is a reason for goodbye

more than a memory
less than a presence

- your last wishes
coveting
       the shell of me

the sun sets
and you breathe fire

meaningless warmth
in the dark

dropping silence

as casual as last night's newspaper
pilfered from the gray-brown carpet
in front of apartment 3b

the colour that
we have been
        becoming

in a riot of addiction
when the surgeon general says
your love causes cancer

but we all die young

harvest

the sky brims with
twilight
  before a storm

when the wind
crosses
cornfields
they ripple in
green silver waves

an ocean
dependant
on the imminent rain

harvested before their time

speechless

your secrets
                              rise

to the surface

 d r i f t w o o d

on a stale sea
of green

of moss
          tumbling from trees

vague strands
        clinging

spiderwebs of promises

woven so carefully into the corner
           no   one

                                    sees

you devour him

intermission

we lie
sipping tea grown cold with time
and your need for conversation

wondering at the dark
and the way your hair gleams under streetlights

reminding me of the hard light of autumn afternoons
the tumble of crimson strands heavy over my palms
like a promise

your skin warmer than the air pressing crisply near

sky like spilled fingerpaint
electric blue hiding behind lemon leaves
that flirt aside under the smoky wind

and im writing
            writing
capturing every elusive moment

i've seen this dream before
i know how it ends

your hand slides free of mine
and i turn to face the empty street
time paused between one moment
and the next

and im still here waiting

sometimes i wonder about the neighbors, she said

we write a song in red
and she buries her face
in the slippery fall of my hair

for inspiration

allowing me to trace the curve of her ear
while she explores my roots

turning, our song falls silent
or does it?

women do not touch
thoughtlessly

i could kiss her for hours because we breathed into each others
mouths

becoming light headed
surfacing for air
plumbing the depths

all i wanted to tame
(a little)
was her heart
not the fragile skin over her pulse
or the helpless freedom of laughter
nor the soft secret places that burn from invasion

we flower
together

maybe tomorrow
you whisper in my ear

my fingers brush your hair,
skin -
hover over your quiet limbs

dust dancing
through unknown currents
of sunlight

shadows stretch
up walls

the tv murmurs in the hallway

you breathe

the scent of dinner
unknowingly

my pen hovers over another white page

(maybe tomorrow)

as you cut the string and spread your wings

sleeping
one arm flung
              carelessly
over your head
i see your heart flutter
like a trapped bird
  fragile blue-white skin
  trembling over the warm pulse
of your life

the world rushes by on sharp heels
striking linoleum
the beep and hiss of machines
that will someday hold you closer than i
in spite of my best efforts
an enemy i cannot fight

but now we are surrounded in numbing quiet -
your breath ghosts out unsupported

and you perch on the balcony from which one day
you will fall
                  or fly
stepping off into
another life

that waits patiently in the wings
with outstretched hands

missing you

unexpected
    grief

remembering
the way you turned just enough under the sun
to block the glare

        (and i forgot to say thank you)

tomorrow, and the day after that

i dream of sharing you
with the world

the way i feel for you
in colours and words

a striking turn of a phrase
and everyone is caught off-guard

a girl i loved once has died
another woman inhabits her body

all the women i have ever touched
merge together
curving into our lovemaking

earthshattering
you marvel in the aftermath

i like you because
you have an affinity for my shadows

i hurt you and you let me
and we don't talk about it

and when you touch me
it is easy to let the world
continue spinning without us

i show you all the women inside me
wanting to explain who i am becoming

you smile, saying you already know

because they came to you while you slept
and asked you to be kind to me

i can’t now, but someday i will
i’ll love you enough to break my heart

maybe someday
i'll whisper brave
  nonsense
against your stillwarm skin and
            break open
under
long fingers

revealing
secrets i know
are better left
unsaid.

you will sleep
peacefully
without missing
what i've stolen from your
            outstretched palms
like so many dreams you
   never
wanted anyway.

the flames of our burning bridges
reflect in your shining eyes

as i am
                scribbled
across your bed
obscene graffiti
    curious eyes can't quite
read.

everything's been complicated
         by our hesitations
and how i can't forget waking
in your arms
with the taste of goodbye
lying heavy on my tongue

your soft tears
making slow sounds
            on my lips.

passionate
         desperation
clenches a velvet fist
around my heart

while i sell your secrets
and my soul
to a bored world
       in long letters

but still you refuse
to give up on me.

the mornings in which i can't wake up
are the hours i dream about you

existing
out there –

in a house by
the sea

skimming the line
between
loneliness
and solitude.

you
possess
a silence

even when
talking to yourself –

writing
singing
carrying on
entire
conversations.

but
in a secret language
there is no laughter to fill
the spaces.

lying still
in the blue-gray dawn
you move in my heart.

the afternoons

in which i can't
wake up

are the stretches when i
         watch sunlight
or stormclouds
              flash and sparkle
implacably

and
wonder
      about

everything between us
     unsaid.

stilted by concern –

the
lines that
              criss-cross

the
desired
weight of words

       a roadmap of
intimacy

                   on a page

          unsent

the evenings in which i can't wake up
are the times when i want to touch you –

                skin warm and breathing –

and tell you not to wait
to be saved.

your world will be quiet

no matter who you people it with

what are you waiting for?
can it be me

of course not.

pencils rattle accusingly
across the floor –

yellow
Ticonderoga
caught in a stray breeze

i retaliate with a pillow
and roll over

there is nothing
to say.

until
midnight when
my fingers remember your number
in the darkness

i blame fate
or inertia
or inevitability

and balance the phone on my
left cheek

closing my eyes through
4 rings
a click
and your waiting silence

at my soft hello

you are saying:
i hate all these neverminds
you keep sending me

i pause
and reply:
sometimes it's enough just to hear your voice

i dream of writing a poem for you

for my mom

i dream of writing a poem for you.
soft pencil scribbles
incomprehensible & beautiful
as if i lead you blindfolded
to paradise
the path is mine alone
but sometimes i want to show you
as pictures: a light
i will never understand why you take everyone's lives so
personally
this, it's chemistry
little parts of me reacting with
you
a volatile experiment
of exquisite precision
the reality that
some things aren't meant to be shared
there are no metaphors for
an edited version of
life.

www.ingramcontent.com/pod-product-compliance
Ingram Content Group UK Ltd.
Pitfield, Milton Keynes, MK11 3LW, UK
UKHW041926190726
13854UKWH00003B/1475

9 781430 312970